# THE POWER *of a* PRAYER

WORDS TO SPEAK AND PRAY

FROM *The Message*

# THE POWER *of a* PRAYER

# EUGENE H. PETERSON

*Bringing Truth to Life*

COLORADO SPRINGS, COLORADO

ISBN 1-57683-722-X

Cover design by: Diana Thornton
Cover photo by Gary Walpole
*The Message* Editorial Team: Terry Behimer, Stephen Board, Darla Hightower, Pat Miller,
    Glynese Northam
*The Power of Prayer* Creative Team: Sarah Snelling, Mindy Mills, Ramona Richards, Darla Hightower,
    Glynese Northam

Published in association with the literary agency of Alive Communications, Inc., 7680 Goddard St., Suite 200, Colorado Springs, CO 80920.

1 2 3 4 5 6 7 8 9 10 11 12 13 14 15 16 17 / 10 09 08 07 06 05

Printed in Canada

# TABLE *of* CONTENTS

*Tab. 92.*

*Kalmia latifolia*
*Die breitblättrige Kalmie.*

Don't fret or worry. Instead of worrying, pray. Let
petitions and praises shape your worries into prayers,
letting God know your concerns. Before you know
it, a sense of God's wholeness, everything coming
together for good, will come and settle you down.

—PHILIPPIANS 4:6-7

# Experience the Power
## *of a* Prayer

From the time we are young, we're taught that prayer is a conversation with God, like a chat with a good friend. But what a friend!

This friend forgives all our mistakes, and no matter what we do or say, he never betrays or leaves us (see Genesis 28:15; Matthew 28:20). How remarkable is it to know that the Creator of the universe will be by our sides at all times, giving us support, love, guidance, and hope — whatever we need. And all we have to do is ask, just as Christ assured us:

> *"Ask and you'll get; seek and you'll find; knock and the door will open. Don't bargain with God. Be direct. Ask for what you need." (Luke 11:9-10)*

Yet prayer is more than a simple conversation, more than requests for our own personal needs or the needs of our loved ones. It is the foundation for the most powerful relationship in our lives: our intimate contact with God. Prayer opens the door to God's mercy and the working of his power in our lives.

The power of prayer is revealed many times in Scripture, from Genesis through the last acts of the apostles. Abraham called on the name of the Lord in Genesis 12, and the church itself was born from one of the most intense prayer meetings in history, described in Acts 2. God's people throughout history have found healing, growth, and provision in the power of prayer. When we give our hearts and minds to God, we open ourselves up to the power to heal, to grow, and to receive God's greatest gifts — or even to change the world.

Yet some people still have difficulty praying. Objections can range from the intimidation factor (you *are* talking to the Creator of the universe) to a lack of knowledge or a lack of time. But be assured that these aren't exactly new excuses; even the Twelve had to be taught how to pray (Luke 11:1-4). And while there are definite benefits to having an extended prayer time set aside during your day, Scripture also says that we should "pray constantly" (Luke 21:36), which means that God should be on our minds all the time, and that it's perfectly all right to say those flashed "byte" prayers during the day, such as asking for God's help for folks in a passing ambulance or a quick request for forgiveness for the language you used in a traffic jam.

As Paul wrote to the troubled Corinthians: "Become friends with God; he's already a friend with you" (2 Corinthians 5:20). There is nothing disrespectful — or unbiblical — about offering up a moment's "Thanks, Lord!" for a beautiful sunrise, or a one-sentence praise for the work he's done in your life recently. And if you think that short prayers aren't effective, remember that it was a very short prayer from Moses that opened the Red Sea and a simple blessing from Jesus that fed five thousand people.

These rapid-fire prayers can also be effective in an unexpected fashion: They can make you more comfortable with the constant — and consistent — presence of God in your life, and help ease you into a fuller prayer life. For these reasons, the verses in this book are kept short. They are meant to share with you some of the most heartfelt prayers of the Bible, show examples of the results of such prayers, and offer moments of reflection intended to inspire prayers in your own life.

The first chapter of the book includes Scriptures that prove how intensely God loves his children and how he is always present, while the second chapter offers up thanks and praise for that astonishing and powerful Presence. The third turns to acts and requests of intercession for our loved ones, and ourselves, so that we all may experience God's love. The fourth focuses on our desires for wisdom and spiritual growth, and the fifth chapter emphasizes our reliance on God for forgiveness, restoration, and renewal in our spirits, minds, and bodies.

The last chapter takes a look at the future — both the immediate future when we will rely on God for all our needs, as well as a time when Christ will welcome us fully into his kingdom. It is a chapter of intense hope and far-reaching dreams.

And it is our hope that you will use the Scriptures in this book as aids to a broader and more beautiful life with God and his Son. A friend recently wrote, "Relationships are the ground where we learn," a sentiment underlined by an understanding that our own prayers can lead us into a deeper union with God, a union truly blessed by the power of his love. All you really have to do is open your heart, and ask.

*Say a quiet yes to God and he'll be there in no time. (James 4:8)*

— THE MESSAGE *Team*

*My response is to get down on my knees
before the Father, this magnificent Father
who parcels out all heaven and earth.*

—EPHESIANS 3:14

Tab. 292.

*Kalmia latifolia*
Die breitblättrige Kalmie

GOD can't stand pious poses,
but he delights in genuine prayers.

— PROVERBS 15:8

# PRAYERS *for* THE POWER *of* GOD IN OUR LIVES

Matthew 18:18-20, *Jesus, describing prayer to his disciples*

"Take this most seriously: A yes on earth is yes in heaven; a no on earth is no in heaven. What you say to one another is eternal. I mean this. When two of you get together on anything at all on earth and make a prayer of it, my Father in heaven goes into action. And when two or three of you are together because of me, you can be sure that I'll be there."

Isaiah 58:9, *Isaiah, speaking to Israel about fasting and repentance*

"Then when you pray, GOD will answer.
     You'll call out for help and I'll say, 'Here I am.'"

Deuteronomy 31:6, *Moses, in his last speech to Israel*

> "Be strong. Take courage. Don't be intimidated. Don't give
> them a second thought because GOD, your God, is striding
> ahead of you. He's right there with you. He won't let you
> down; he won't leave you."

1 Kings 8:22-24

> Before the entire congregation of Israel, Solomon took
> a position before the Altar, spread his hands out before
> heaven, and prayed, O GOD, God of Israel, there is no
> God like you in the skies above or on the earth below who
> unswervingly keeps covenant with his servants and relent-
> lessly loves them as they sincerely live in obedience to your
> way. You kept your word to David my father, your personal
> word. You did exactly what you promised — every detail.

Matthew 11:25-26

> Abruptly Jesus broke into prayer: "Thank you, Father, Lord
> of heaven and earth. You've concealed your ways from
> sophisticates and know-it-alls, but spelled them out clearly to
> ordinary people. Yes, Father, that's the way you like to work."

Exodus 15:11, *Moses and Israel, joined in a prayer song of praise*

> Who compares with you
>> among gods, O GOD?
> Who compares with you in power,
>> in holy majesty,
> In awesome praises,
>> wonder-working God?

1 Thessalonians 5:24-26

> The One who called you is completely dependable. If he said it, he'll do it!
> Friends, keep up your prayers for us. Greet all the Christians there with a holy embrace.

Psalm 6:9

> My requests have all been granted,
>> my prayers are answered.

Acts 8:14-17

> When the apostles in Jerusalem received the report that
> Samaria had accepted God's Message, they sent Peter and
> John down to pray for them to receive the Holy Spirit. Up
> to this point they had only been baptized in the name of
> the Master Jesus; the Holy Spirit hadn't yet fallen on them.
> Then the apostles laid their hands on them and they did
> receive the Holy Spirit.

Matthew 6:6, *Jesus, with instructions on how to pray*

> "Here's what I want you to do: Find a quiet, secluded place
> so you won't be tempted to role-play before God. Just be
> there as simply and honestly as you can manage. The focus
> will shift from you to God, and you will begin to sense his
> grace."

Psalm 13:2-6

> Take a good look at me, GOD, my God;
>     I want to look life in the eye,
> So no enemy can get the best of me
>     or laugh when I fall on my face.

I've thrown myself headlong into your arms —
    I'm celebrating your rescue.
I'm singing at the top of my lungs,
    I'm so full of answered prayers.

Deuteronomy 10:12-18, *Moses, to Israel, on how to honor God*

So now Israel, what do you think GOD expects from you? Just this: Live in his presence in holy reverence, follow the road he sets out for you, love him, serve GOD, your God, with everything you have in you, obey the commandments and regulations of GOD that I'm commanding you today — live a good life.

Look around you: Everything you see is GOD's — the heavens above and beyond, the Earth, and everything on it. But it was your ancestors that GOD fell in love with; he picked their children — that's *you!* — out of all the other peoples. That's where we are right now. So cut away the thick calluses from your heart and stop being so willfully hardheaded. GOD, your God, is the God of all gods, he's the Master of all masters, a God immense and powerful and awesome. He doesn't play favorites, takes no bribes, makes

sure orphans and widows are treated fairly, takes loving care
of foreigners by seeing that they get food and clothing.

John 17:1-5

Jesus said these things. Then, raising his eyes in prayer, he said:

"Father, it's time.
Display the bright splendor of your Son
So the Son in turn may show your bright splendor.
You put him in charge of everything human
So he might give real and eternal life to all in his charge.
And this is the real and eternal life:
That they know you,
The one and only true God,
And Jesus Christ, whom you sent.
I glorified you on earth
By completing down to the last detail
What you assigned me to do.
And now, Father, glorify me with your very own splendor,
The very splendor I had in your presence
Before there was a world."

Acts 7:32-33, *Stephen, speaking of God's presence with Israel throughout history*

> "'I am the God of your fathers, the God of Abraham, Isaac, and Jacob.' Frightened nearly out of his skin, Moses shut his eyes and turned away."

> "God said, 'Kneel and pray. You are in a holy place, on holy ground. I've seen the agony of my people in Egypt. I've heard their groans. I've come to help them.'"

Psalm 71:17-19

> You got me when I was an unformed youth,
>> God, and taught me everything I know.
> Now I'm telling the world your wonders;
>> I'll keep at it until I'm old and gray.
> God, don't walk off and leave me
>> until I get out the news
> Of your strong right arm to this world,
>> news of your power to the world yet to come,
> Your famous and righteous
>> ways, O God.
> God, you've done it all!
>> Who is quite like you?

James 5:11

> What a gift life is to those who stay the course! You've
> heard, of course, of Job's staying power, and you know
> how God brought it all together for him at the end. That's
> because God cares, cares right down to the last detail.

Psalm 34:6-8

> When I was desperate, I called out,
> and GOD got me out of a tight spot.
>
> GOD's angel sets up a circle
> of protection around us while we pray.
>
> Open your mouth and taste, open your eyes and see —
>    how good GOD is.
> Blessed are you who run to him.

Acts 4:31-32

> While they were praying, the place where they were meet-
> ing trembled and shook. They were all filled with the Holy
> Spirit and continued to speak God's Word with fearless
> confidence.

The whole congregation of believers was united as one — one heart, one mind!

Matthew 26:41, *Jesus, to Peter, in the Garden of Gethsemane*

"Stay alert; be in prayer so you don't wander into temptation without even knowing you're in danger. There is a part of you that is eager, ready for anything in God. But there's another part that's as lazy as an old dog sleeping by the fire."

Psalm 89:1-2

Your love, GOD, is my song, and I'll sing it!
    I'm forever telling everyone how faithful you are.
I'll never quit telling the story of your love —
    how you built the cosmos
    and guaranteed everything in it.
Your love has always been our lives' foundation,
    your fidelity has been the roof over our world.

Daniel 9:23, *Gabriel, to Daniel, with a message from God*

> "'You had no sooner started your prayer when the answer
> was given. And now I'm here to deliver the answer to you.
> You are much loved!'"

Habakkuk 3:2

> GOD, I've heard what our ancestors say about you,
> > and I'm stopped in my tracks, down on my knees.
> Do among us what you did among them.
> > Work among us as you worked among them.
> And as you bring judgment, as you surely must,
> > remember mercy.

Romans 8:25-27

> But the longer we wait, the larger we become, and the more
> joyful our expectancy.
> > Meanwhile, the moment we get tired in the waiting,
> God's Spirit is right alongside helping us along. If we don't
> know how or what to pray, it doesn't matter. He does our
> praying in and for us, making prayer out of our wordless

sighs, our aching groans. He knows us far better than we know ourselves, knows our pregnant condition, and keeps us present before God.

Matthew 5:43-45, *Jesus, in the Sermon on the Mount*

"You're familiar with the old written law, 'Love your friend,' and its unwritten companion, 'Hate your enemy.' I'm challenging that. I'm telling you to love your enemies. Let them bring out the best in you, not the worst. When someone gives you a hard time, respond with the energies of prayer, for then you are working out of your true selves, your God-created selves. This is what God does. He gives his best — the sun to warm and the rain to nourish — to everyone, regardless: the good and bad, the nice and nasty."

Acts 10:30-33

Cornelius said, "Four days ago at about this time, mid-afternoon, I was home praying. Suddenly there was a man right in front of me, flooding the room with light. He said, 'Cornelius, your daily prayers and neighborly acts have brought you to God's attention. I want you to send to

Joppa to get Simon, the one they call Peter. He's staying
with Simon the Tanner down by the sea.'

"So I did it — I sent for you. And you've been good enough
to come. And now we're all here in God's presence, ready to
listen to whatever the Master put in your heart to tell us."

Matthew 22:36-37

"Teacher, which command in God's Law is the most
important?"

Jesus said, "'Love the Lord your God with all your pas-
sion and prayer and intelligence.' This is the most important, the first on any list."

Luke 3:21-22

After all the people were baptized, Jesus was baptized. As
he was praying, the sky opened up and the Holy Spirit, like
a dove descending, came down on him. And along with the
Spirit, a voice: "You are my Son, chosen and marked by my
love, pride of my life."

Acts 16:24-26

> He did just that — threw them into the maximum security
> cell in the jail and clamped leg irons on them.
>
> Along about midnight, Paul and Silas were at prayer
> and singing a robust hymn to God. The other prisoners
> couldn't believe their ears. Then, without warning, a huge
> earthquake! The jailhouse tottered, every door flew open,
> all the prisoners were loose.

2 Corinthians 1:10-11

> And he did it, rescued us from certain doom. *And* he'll do it
> again, rescuing us as many times as we need rescuing. You
> and your prayers are part of the rescue operation — I don't
> want you in the dark about that either. I can see your faces
> even now, lifted in praise for God's deliverance of us, a
> rescue in which your prayers played such a crucial part.

Acts 2:41-42, *Peter, speaking in the Upper Room after the coming of the Holy Spirit*

> That day about three thousand took him at his word, were
> baptized and were signed up. They committed themselves to

the teaching of the apostles, the life together, the common meal, and the prayers.

Everyone around was in awe — all those wonders and signs done through the apostles!

Romans 8:10-11

But for you who welcome him, in whom he dwells — even though you still experience all the limitations of sin — you yourself experience life on God's terms. It stands to reason, doesn't it, that if the alive-and-present God who raised Jesus from the dead moves into your life, he'll do the same thing in you that he did in Jesus, bringing you alive to himself? When God lives and breathes in you (and he does, as surely as he did in Jesus), you are delivered from that dead life. With his Spirit living in you, your body will be as alive as Christ's!

*Let's take our place outside with Jesus,*

*no longer pouring out the sacrificial blood*

*of animals but pouring out sacrificial praises*

*from our lips to God in Jesus' name.*

—HEBREWS 13:15

GOD *keeps his distance from the wicked;*

*he closely attends to the prayers of God-loyal people.*

—PROVERBS 15:29

# PRAYERS *of*
# THANKS AND PRAISE

1 Timothy 4:4-6

> Everything God created is good, and to be received with thanks. Nothing is to be sneered at and thrown out. God's Word and our prayers make every item in creation holy.
>
> You've been raised on the Message of the faith and have followed sound teaching. Now pass on this counsel to the Christians there, and you'll be a good servant of Jesus.

1 Chronicles 16:33-36, *a praise of David's before the chest of God*

> Then the trees in the forest will add their applause
>   to all who are pleased and present before GOD
>   — he's on his way to set things right!

Give thanks to GOD — he is good
>    and his love never quits.
Say, "Save us, Savior God,
>    round us up and get us out of these godless places,
So we can give thanks to your holy Name,
>    and bask in your life of praise."
Blessed be GOD, the God of Israel,
>    from everlasting to everlasting.


Then everybody said, "Yes! Amen!" and "Praise GOD!"

## 2 Thessalonians 2:13-14

Meanwhile, we've got our hands full continually thanking God for you, our good friends—so loved by God! God
picked you out as his from the very start. Think of it:
included in God's original plan of salvation by the bond
of faith in the living truth. This is the life of the Spirit he
invited you to through the Message we delivered, in which
you get in on the glory of our Master, Jesus Christ.

Psalm 149:1-4

> Hallelujah!
> Sing to GOD a brand-new song,
>> praise him in the company of all who love him.
> Let all Israel celebrate their Sovereign Creator,
>> Zion's children exult in their King.
> Let them praise his name in dance;
>> strike up the band and make great music!
> And why? Because GOD delights in his people,
>> festoons plain folk with salvation garlands!

Acts 4:23-24

> As soon as Peter and John were let go, they went to their
> friends and told them what the high priests and religious
> leaders had said. Hearing the report, they lifted their voices
> in a wonderful harmony in prayer: "Strong God, you made
> heaven and earth and sea and everything in them."

1 Chronicles 29:12-14, *prayer of David, after receiving gifts for the Temple*

> Riches and glory come from you,
>> you're ruler over all;

You hold strength and power in the palm of your hand
to build up and strengthen all.
And here we are, O God, our God, giving thanks to you,
praising your splendid Name.

"But me — who am I, and who are these my people, that we
should presume to be giving something to you? Everything
comes from you; all we're doing is giving back what we've
been given from your generous hand."

1 Thessalonians 5:17-18

Pray all the time; thank God no matter what happens.
This is the way God wants you who belong to Christ Jesus
to live.

Acts 28:14-15

We found Christian friends there and stayed with them for
a week.
And then we came to Rome. Friends in Rome heard
we were on the way and came out to meet us. One group
got as far as Appian Court; another group met us at Three

Taverns — emotion-packed meetings, as you can well imagine. Paul, brimming over with praise, led us in prayers of thanksgiving.

1 Thessalonians 2:11-13

You experienced it all firsthand. With each of you we were like a father with his child, holding your hand, whispering encouragement, showing you step-by-step how to live well before God, who called us into his own kingdom, into this delightful life.

And now we look back on all this and thank God, an artesian well of thanks! When you got the Message of God we preached, you didn't pass it off as just one more human opinion, but you took it to heart as God's true word to you, which it is, God himself at work in you believers!

Psalm 30:1-4

I give you all the credit, GOD —
      you got me out of that mess,
      you didn't let my foes gloat.

GOD, my God, I yelled for help
    and you put me together.
GOD, you pulled me out of the grave,
    gave me another chance at life
    when I was down-and-out.

All you saints! Sing your hearts out to GOD!
    Thank him to his face!

1 Corinthians 14:25-26

Probe their hearts. Before you know it, they're going to be on their faces before God, recognizing that God is among you.

So here's what I want you to do. When you gather for worship, each one of you be prepared with something that will be useful for all: Sing a hymn, teach a lesson, tell a story, lead a prayer, provide an insight.

Psalm 66:1-3

All together now—applause for God!
    Sing songs to the tune of his glory,
    set glory to the rhythms of his praise.
Say of God, "We've never seen anything like him!"

1 Peter 2:9-10

> But you are the ones chosen by God, chosen for the
> high calling of priestly work, chosen to be a holy people,
> God's instruments to do his work and speak out for him,
> to tell others of the night-and-day difference he made
> for you — from nothing to something, from rejected to
> accepted.

2 Corinthians 9:14-15

> Meanwhile, moved by the extravagance of God in your lives,
> they'll respond by praying for you in passionate intercession
> for whatever you need. Thank God for this gift, his gift. No
> language can praise it enough!

Ephesians 3:20-21

> God can do anything, you know — far more than you could
> ever imagine or guess or request in your wildest dreams! He
> does it not by pushing us around but by working within us,
> his Spirit deeply and gently within us.
>
> > Glory to God in the church!
> > Glory to God in the Messiah, in Jesus!

Glory down all the generations!
Glory through all millennia! Oh, yes!

Psalm 56:10-13

I'm proud to praise God,
    proud to praise GOD.
Fearless now, I trust in God;
    what can mere mortals do to me?

God, you did everything you promised,
    and I'm thanking you with all my heart.
You pulled me from the brink of death,
    my feet from the cliff-edge of doom.
Now I stroll at leisure with God
    in the sunlit fields of life.

1 Thessalonians 1:2-3

Every time we think of you, we thank God for you. Day and
night you're in our prayers as we call to mind your work of
faith, your labor of love, and your patience of hope in following our Master, Jesus Christ, before God our Father.

Genesis 26:24-25

That very night GOD appeared to him and said,

> I am the God of Abraham your father;
>    don't fear a thing because I'm with you.
> I'll bless you and make your children flourish
>    because of Abraham my servant.

Isaac built an altar there and prayed, calling on GOD by name. He pitched his tent and his servants started digging another well.

Matthew 8:4

Jesus said, "Don't talk about this all over town. Just quietly present your healed body to the priest, along with the appropriate expressions of thanks to God. Your cleansed and grateful life, not your words, will bear witness to what I have done."

Psalm 119:61-63

> The wicked hemmed me in — there was no way out —
>> but not for a minute did I forget your plan for me.
> I get up in the middle of the night to thank you;
>> your decisions are so right, so true — I can't wait till
>>> morning!
> I'm a friend and companion of all who fear you,
>> of those committed to living by your rules.

Ephesians 1:15-17

> That's why, when I heard of the solid trust you have in
> the Master Jesus and your outpouring of love to all the
> Christians, I couldn't stop thanking God for you—every
> time I prayed, I'd think of you and give thanks. But I do
> more than thank. I ask — ask the God of our Master, Jesus
> Christ, the God of glory — to make you intelligent and
> discerning in knowing him personally.

2 Samuel 7:18-21

> King David went in, took his place before GOD, and prayed:
> "Who am I, my Master GOD, and what is my family, that

you have brought me to this place in life? But that's nothing
compared to what's coming, for you've also spoken of my
family far into the future, given me a glimpse into tomor-
row, my Master GOD! What can I possibly say in the face
of all this? You know me, Master GOD, just as I am. You've
done all this not because of who I am but because of who
you are—out of your very heart!"

Philippians 1:3-5

Every time you cross my mind, I break out in exclamations
of thanks to God. Each exclamation is a trigger to prayer.
I find myself praying for you with a glad heart. I am so
pleased that you have continued on in this with us, believ-
ing and proclaiming God's Message, from the day you heard
it right up to the present.

Isaiah 12:3-5

Joyfully you'll pull up buckets of water
        from the wells of salvation.
And as you do it, you'll say,
        "Give thanks to GOD.

Call out his name.

Ask him anything!

Shout to the nations, tell them what he's done,

spread the news of his great reputation!

"Sing praise-songs to GOD. He's done it all!

Let the whole earth know what he's done!"

2 Samuel 22:1-3

David prayed to GOD the words of this song after GOD
saved him from all his enemies and from Saul.

GOD is bedrock under my feet,

the castle in which I live,

my rescuing knight.

My God — the high crag

where I run for dear life,

hiding behind the boulders,

safe in the granite hideout;

My mountaintop refuge.

Psalm 28:6-7

> Blessed be GOD —
>> he heard me praying.
> He proved he's on my side;
>> I've thrown my lot in with him.
>
> Now I'm jumping for joy,
>> and shouting and singing my thanks to him.

Psalm 109:30-31

> My mouth's full of great praise for GOD,
>> I'm singing his hallelujahs surrounded by crowds,
> For he's always at hand to take the side of the needy,
>> to rescue a life from the unjust judge.

Psalm 105:1-2

> Hallelujah!
>
> Thank GOD! Pray to him by name!
>> Tell everyone you meet what he has done!
> Sing him songs, belt out hymns,
>> translate his wonders into music!

1 Samuel 2:1-10, *Hannah's prayer when she dedicated her son Samuel to God*

> Hannah prayed:
>
> I'm bursting with God-news!
>> I'm walking on air.
> I'm laughing at my rivals.
>> I'm dancing my salvation.
>
> Nothing and no one is holy like GOD,
>> no rock mountain like our God.
> Don't dare talk pretentiously—
>> not a word of boasting, ever!
> For GOD knows what's going on.
>> He takes the measure of everything that happens.
> The weapons of the strong are smashed to pieces,
>> while the weak are infused with fresh strength.
> The well-fed are out begging in the streets for crusts,
>> while the hungry are getting second helpings.
> The barren woman has a houseful of children,
>> while the mother of many is bereft.

GOD brings death and GOD brings life,
>   brings down to the grave and raises up.
GOD brings poverty and GOD brings wealth;
>   he lowers, he also lifts up.
He puts poor people on their feet again;
>   he rekindles burned-out lives with fresh hope,
Restoring dignity and respect to their lives—
>   a place in the sun!
For the very structures of earth are GOD's;
>   he has laid out his operations on a firm foundation.
He protectively cares for his faithful friends, step by step,
>   but leaves the wicked to stumble in the dark.
>   No one makes it in this life by sheer muscle!
GOD's enemies will be blasted out of the sky,
>   crashed in a heap and burned.
GOD will set things right all over the earth,
>   he'll give strength to his king,
>   he'll set his anointed on top of the world!

"That's why I urge you to pray for absolutely
everything, ranging from small to large.
Include everything as you embrace this God-life,
and you'll get God's everything."

—Mark 11:24

# PRAYERS *for* FRIENDS, FAMILY, AND PERSONAL DESIRES

Matthew 6:8-10

"Don't fall for that nonsense. This is your Father you are dealing with, and he knows better than you what you need. With a God like this loving you, you can pray very simply. Like this:

Our Father in heaven,
Reveal who you are.
Set the world right;
Do what's best —
    as above, so below."

Hebrews 13:18-19

> Pray for us. We have no doubts about what we're doing or why, but it's hard going and we need your prayers. All we care about is living well before God. Pray that we may be together soon.

Psalm 34:17

> Is anyone crying for help?
> GOD is listening, ready to rescue you.

Luke 1:12-14

> Zachariah was paralyzed in fear.
> But the angel reassured him, "Don't fear, Zachariah. Your prayer has been heard. Elizabeth, your wife, will bear a son by you. You are to name him John. You're going to leap like a gazelle for joy, and not only you—many will delight in his birth."

2 Samuel 7:22,25,27-29, *a prayer of David, after Nathan tells him of the vision of the Temple and the blessing on David's family*

> "This is what makes you so great, Master GOD! There is none like you, no God but you, nothing to compare with

what we've heard with our own ears. . . .

"So now, great GOD, this word that you have spoken to me and my family, guarantee it permanently! Do exactly what you've promised! . . . For you, GOD-of-the-Angel-Armies, Israel's God, told me plainly, 'I will build you a house.' That's how I was able to find the courage to pray this prayer to you.

"And now, Master GOD, being the God you are, speaking sure words as you do, and having just said this wonderful thing to me, please, just one more thing: Bless my family; keep your eye on them always. You've already as much as said that you would, Master GOD! Oh, may your blessing be on my family permanently!"

3 John 1-3

The Pastor, to my good friend Gaius: How truly I love you! We're the best of friends, and I pray for good fortune in everything you do, and for your good health — that your everyday affairs prosper, as well as your soul! I was most happy when some friends arrived and brought the news that you persist in following the way of Truth.

James 5:16

> Make this your common practice: Confess your sins to each
> other and pray for each other so that you can live together
> whole and healed. The prayer of a person living right with
> God is something powerful to be reckoned with.

Luke 12:29-32, *Jesus, instructing his disciples on how God provides all our needs*

> "Steep yourself in God-reality, God-initiative, God-provisions.
> You'll find all your everyday human concerns will be met.
> Don't be afraid of missing out. You're my dearest friends! The
> Father wants to give you the very kingdom itself."

Romans 10:1

> Believe me, friends, all I want for Israel is what's best for
> Israel: salvation, nothing less. I want it with all my heart
> and pray to God for it all the time.

John 17:9-11, *Jesus, praying for his friends*

> "I pray for them.
> I'm not praying for the God-rejecting world

But for those you gave me,

For they are yours by right.

Everything mine is yours, and yours mine,

And my life is on display in them.

For I'm no longer going to be visible in the world;

They'll continue in the world

While I return to you.

Holy Father, guard them as they pursue this life

That you conferred as a gift through me,

So they can be one heart and mind."

Psalm 115:14-15

Oh, let GOD enlarge your families —

giving growth to you, growth to your children.

May you be blessed by GOD,

by GOD, who made heaven and earth.

1 Corinthians 14:5

I want all of you to develop intimacies with God in prayer,
but please don't stop with that. Go on and proclaim his
clear truth to others.

Colossians 1:3

> Our prayers for you are always spilling over into thanksgivings. We can't quit thanking God our Father and Jesus our Messiah for you!

Genesis 17:19-20

> But God said, "That's not what I mean. Your wife, Sarah, will have a baby, a son. Name him Isaac (Laughter). I'll establish my covenant with him and his descendants, a covenant that lasts forever.
>
> "And Ishmael? Yes, I heard your prayer for him. I'll also bless him; I'll make sure he has plenty of children — a huge family. He'll father twelve princes; I'll make him a great nation."

Acts 12:5-7,12

> All the time that Peter was under heavy guard in the jailhouse, the church prayed for him most strenuously.
>
> Then the time came for Herod to bring him out for the kill. That night, even though shackled to two soldiers, one on either side, Peter slept like a baby. And there were

guards at the door keeping their eyes on the place. Herod was taking no chances!

Suddenly there was an angel at his side and light flooding the room. The angel shook Peter and got him up: "Hurry!" The handcuffs fell off his wrists. . . .

Still shaking his head, amazed, he went to Mary's house, the Mary who was John Mark's mother. The house was packed with praying friends.

1 Chronicles 4:9-10

Jabez was a better man than his brothers, a man of honor. His mother had named him Jabez (Oh, the pain!), saying, "A painful birth! I bore him in great pain!" Jabez prayed to the God of Israel: "Bless me, O bless me! Give me land, large tracts of land. And provide your personal protection — don't let evil hurt me." God gave him what he asked.

2 Thessalonians 3:1

One more thing, friends: Pray for us. Pray that the Master's Word will simply take off and race through the country to a groundswell of response, just as it did among you.

Ezra 8:21-22

> I proclaimed a fast there beside the Ahava Canal, a fast to humble ourselves before our God and pray for wise guidance for our journey — all our people and possessions. I was embarrassed to ask the king for a cavalry bodyguard to protect us from bandits on the road. We had just told the king, "Our God lovingly looks after all those who seek him, but turns away in disgust from those who leave him."

1 Timothy 1:18-19

> I'm passing this work on to you, my son Timothy. The prophetic word that was directed to you prepared us for this. All those prayers are coming together now so you will do this well, fearless in your struggle, keeping a firm grip on your faith and on yourself. After all, this is a fight we're in.

Acts 20:31-32, *Paul, to the leaders of the Ephesus congregation*

> "So stay awake and keep up your guard. Remember those three years I kept at it with you, never letting up, pouring my heart out with you, one after another.

"Now I'm turning you over to God, our marvelous God whose gracious Word can make you into what he wants you to be and give you everything you could possibly need in this community of holy friends."

Colossians 4:12-13

Epaphras, who is one of you, says hello. What a trooper he has been! He's been tireless in his prayers for you, praying that you'll stand firm, mature and confident in everything God wants you to do. I've watched him closely, and can report on how hard he has worked for you and for those in Laodicea and Hierapolis.

Job 22:26-28

"You'll take delight in God, the Mighty One,
and look to him joyfully, boldly.
You'll pray to him and he'll listen;
he'll help you do what you've promised.
You'll decide what you want and it will happen;
your life will be bathed in light."

Philippians 4:10-11

> I'm glad in God, far happier than you would ever guess —
> happy that you're again showing such strong concern for
> me. Not that you ever quit praying and thinking about me.
> You just had no chance to show it. Actually, I don't have a
> sense of needing anything personally. I've learned by now to
> be quite content whatever my circumstances.

Psalm 105:40-42

> They prayed and he brought quail,
>     filled them with the bread of heaven;
> He opened the rock and water poured out;
>     it flowed like a river through that desert —
> All because he remembered his Covenant,
>     his promise to Abraham, his servant.

Philemon 3-7

> God's best to you! Christ's blessings on you!
>     Every time your name comes up in my prayers, I say,
> "Oh, thank you, God!" I keep hearing of the love and faith
> you have for the Master Jesus, which brims over to other

Christians. And I keep praying that this faith we hold in common keeps showing up in the good things we do, and that people recognize Christ in all of it. Friend, you have no idea how good your love makes me feel, doubly so when I see your hospitality to fellow believers.

2 Timothy 1:2-4

I write this to you, Timothy, the son I love so much. All the best from our God and Christ be yours!

Every time I say your name in prayer — which is practically all the time — I thank God for you, the God I worship with my whole life in the tradition of my ancestors. I miss you a lot, especially when I remember that last tearful good-bye, and I look forward to a joy-packed reunion.

Colossians 4:2-4

Pray diligently. Stay alert, with your eyes wide open in gratitude. Don't forget to pray for us, that God will open doors for telling the mystery of Christ, even while I'm locked up in this jail. Pray that every time I open my mouth I'll be able to make Christ plain as day to them.

1 Samuel 22:14-15, *Ahimelech's response, when Saul accused him of conspiring with David*

> Ahimelech answered the king, "There's not an official in your administration as true to you as David, your own son-in-law and captain of your bodyguard. None more honorable either. Do you think that was the first time I prayed with him for God's guidance? Hardly!"

Philippians 1:8-11

> Sometimes I think I feel as strongly about you as Christ does!
>
> So this is my prayer: that your love will flourish and that you will not only love much but well. Learn to love appropriately. You need to use your head and test your feelings so that your love is sincere and intelligent, not sentimental gush. Live a lover's life, circumspect and exemplary, a life Jesus will be proud of: bountiful in fruits from the soul, making Jesus Christ attractive to all, getting everyone involved in the glory and praise of God.

Romans 1:9-11

And God, whom I so love to worship and serve by spreading the good news of his Son — the Message! — knows that every time I think of you in my prayers, which is practically all the time, I ask him to clear the way for me to come and see you. The longer this waiting goes on, the deeper the ache. I so want to be there to deliver God's gift in person and watch you grow stronger right before my eyes!

Genesis 16:11-13

"From this pregnancy, you'll get a son: Name him Ishmael;
    for GOD heard you, GOD answered you.
He'll be a bucking bronco of a man,
    a real fighter, fighting and being fought,
Always stirring up trouble,
    always at odds with his family."

She answered GOD by name, praying to the God who spoke to her, "You're the God who sees me!"
"Yes! He saw me; and then I saw him!"

Romans 15:29

> My hope is that my visit with you is going to be one of
> Christ's more extravagant blessings.
>     I have one request, dear friends: Pray for me. Pray stren-
> uously with and for me — to God the Father, through the
> power of our Master Jesus, through the love of the Spirit.

Psalm 39:12-13

> "Ah, GOD, listen to my prayer, my
>     cry—open your ears.
> Don't be callous;
>     just look at these tears of mine.
> I'm a stranger here. I don't know my way—
>     a migrant like my whole family.
> Give me a break, cut me some slack
>     before it's too late and I'm out of here."

Psalms 61:1

> God, listen to me shout,
>     bend an ear to my prayer.

*Whatever I have, wherever I am,*
*I can make it through anything*
*in the One who makes me who I am.*

—Philippians 4:13

*Hibiscus syriacus flore variegato.*
*Die gerfilbe Hospsstrauch mit schöppeter Blüthe.*

*Bless my family. Keep your eye on them always.*
*You've already as much as said that you would,*
*Master GOD! Oh, may your blessing be on*
*my family permanently!"*

—2 SAMUEL 7:29

# Prayers *for* Wisdom, Strength, and Guidance

Proverbs 3:5-6, *Solomon, on listening for God's answers to prayer*

> Trust GOD from the bottom of your heart;
>> don't try to figure out everything on your own.
> Listen for GOD's voice in everything you do, everywhere you go;
>> he's the one who will keep you on track.

Nehemiah 6:8-9, *Nehemiah, after Sanballat accused the Jews of rebuilding the wall so that they could rebel*

> I sent him back this: "There's nothing to what you're saying. You've made it all up."
>
> They were trying to intimidate us into quitting. They thought, "They'll give up; they'll never finish it."
>
> I prayed, "Give me strength."

Hebrews 5:7-8

> While he lived on earth, anticipating death, Jesus cried out
> in pain and wept in sorrow as he offered up priestly prayers
> to God. Because he honored God, God answered him.
> Though he was God's Son, he learned trusting-obedience
> by what he suffered, just as we do.

Psalm 119:26-27

> When I told my story, you responded;
>     train me well in your deep wisdom.
> Help me understand these things inside and out
>     so I can ponder your miracle-wonders.

Jeremiah 32:17-19

> "'Dear GOD, my Master, you created earth and sky by your
> great power—by merely stretching out your arm! There is
> nothing you can't do. You're loyal in your steadfast love to
> thousands upon thousands—but you also make children live
> with the fallout from their parents' sins. Great and power-
> ful God, named GOD-of-the-Angel-Armies, determined
> in purpose and relentless in following through, you see

everything that men and women do and respond appropriately to the way they live, to the things they do.'"

## Job 37:23-24

"Mighty God! Far beyond our reach!
  Unsurpassable in power and justice!
  It's unthinkable that he'd treat anyone unfairly.
So bow to him in deep reverence, one and all!
  If you're wise, you'll most certainly worship him."

## 2 Timothy 1:5-7

That precious memory triggers another: your honest faith—and what a rich faith it is, handed down from your grandmother Lois to your mother Eunice, and now to you! And the special gift of ministry you received when I laid hands on you and prayed—keep that ablaze! God doesn't want us to be shy with his gifts, but bold and loving and sensible.

## 2 Chronicles 1:11-12

God answered Solomon, "This is what has come out of your heart: You didn't grasp for money, wealth, fame, and the doom of your enemies; you didn't even ask for a long life. You asked for wisdom and knowledge so you could govern well my people over whom I've made you king. Because of this, you get what you asked for — wisdom and knowledge. And I'm presenting you the rest as a bonus — money, wealth, and fame beyond anything the kings before or after you had or will have."

Jeremiah 9:23-24, *God answers Jeremiah's prayerful grief over Judah's sins*

GOD's Message:

"Don't let the wise brag of their wisdom.
    Don't let heroes brag of their exploits.
Don't let the rich brag of their riches.
    If you brag, brag of this and this only:
That you understand and know me.
    I'm GOD, and I act in loyal love.
I do what's right and set things right and fair,
    and delight in those who do the same things.
These are my trademarks."

## 1 Timothy 2:1-3

The first thing I want you to do is pray. Pray every way you
know how, for everyone you know. Pray especially for rulers
and their governments to rule well so we can be quietly about
our business of living simply, in humble contemplation. This
is the way our Savior God wants us to live.

## Lamentations 3:28-29

When life is heavy and hard to take,
   go off by yourself. Enter the silence.
Bow in prayer. Don't ask questions:
   Wait for hope to appear.

## Colossians 1:9-12

Be assured that from the first day we heard of you, we
haven't stopped praying for you, asking God to give you
wise minds and spirits attuned to his will, and so acquire
a thorough understanding of the ways in which God
works. We pray that you'll live well for the Master, mak-
ing him proud of you as you work hard in his orchard.
As you learn more and more how God works, you will

learn how to do *your* work. We pray that you'll have the strength to stick it out over the long haul — not the grim strength of gritting your teeth but the glory-strength God gives. It is strength that endures the unendurable and spills over into joy, thanking the Father who makes us strong enough to take part in everything bright and beautiful that he has for us.

1 Peter 4:6-8

Listen to the Message. It was preached to those believers who are now dead, and yet even though they died (just as all people must), they will still get in on the *life* that God has given in Jesus.

Everything in the world is about to be wrapped up, so take nothing for granted. Stay wide-awake in prayer. Most of all, love each other as if your life depended on it. Love makes up for practically anything.

Luke 22:31-32

"Simon, stay on your toes. Satan has tried his best to separate all of you from me, like chaff from wheat. Simon, I've prayed for you in particular that you not give in or give out. When you have come through the time of testing, turn to your companions and give them a fresh start."

2 Corinthians 13:8-9

We're rooting for the truth to win out in you. We couldn't possibly do otherwise.

We don't just put up with our limitations; we celebrate them, and then go on to celebrate every strength, every triumph of the truth in you. We pray hard that it will all come together in your lives.

1 Timothy 2:7-8

This and this only has been my appointed work: getting this news to those who have never heard of God, and explaining how it works by simple faith and plain truth.

Since prayer is at the bottom of all this, what I want mostly is for men to pray — not shaking angry fists at enemies but raising holy hands to God.

Romans 12:11-12

> Don't burn out; keep yourselves fueled and aflame. Be alert
> servants of the Master, cheerfully expectant. Don't quit in
> hard times; pray all the harder.

James 1:5-6

> If you don't know what you're doing, pray to the Father. He
> loves to help. You'll get his help, and won't be condescended
> to when you ask for it. Ask boldly, believingly, without a
> second thought.

Luke 21:36

> "So, whatever you do, don't go to sleep at the switch. Pray
> constantly that you will have the strength and wits to make
> it through everything that's coming and end up on your feet
> before the Son of Man."

1 Corinthians 14:15

> So what's the solution? The answer is simple enough. Do
> both. I should be spiritually free and expressive as I pray,

but I should also be thoughtful and mindful as I pray. I should sing with my spirit, and sing with my mind.

1 Chronicles 5:20

God helped them as they fought. God handed the Hagrites and all their allies over to them, because they cried out to him during the battle. God answered their prayers because they trusted him.

Acts 20:35-37

"In everything I've done, I have demonstrated to you how necessary it is to work on behalf of the weak and not exploit them. You'll not likely go wrong here if you keep remembering that our Master said, 'You're far happier giving than getting.'"

Then Paul went down on his knees, all of them kneeling with him, and prayed. And then a river of tears. Much clinging to Paul, not wanting to let him go.

2 Timothy 2:21-23

Become the kind of container God can use to present any and every kind of gift to his guests for their blessing.

Run away from infantile indulgence. Run after mature righteousness — faith, love, peace — joining those who are in honest and serious prayer before God. Refuse to get involved in inane discussions; they always end up in fights.

Ephesians 6:14-20

Truth, righteousness, peace, faith, and salvation are more than words. Learn how to apply them. You'll need them throughout your life. God's Word is an *indispensable* weapon. In the same way, prayer is essential in this ongoing warfare. Pray hard and long. Pray for your brothers and sisters. Keep your eyes open. Keep each other's spirits up so that no one falls behind or drops out.

And don't forget to pray for me. Pray that I'll know what to say and have the courage to say it at the right time, telling the mystery to one and all, the Message that I, jail-bird preacher that I am, am responsible for getting out.

Mark 14:38

"Stay alert, be in prayer, so you don't enter the danger zone without even knowing it. Don't be naive. Part of you is eager, ready for anything in God; but another part is as lazy as an old dog sleeping by the fire."

*May God himself, the God who makes
everything holy and whole, make you holy
and whole, put you together—spirit, soul,
and body—and keep you fit for the coming
of our Master, Jesus Christ.*

—1 THESSALONIANS 5:23

# Prayers *for*
# Forgiveness and Healing

Matthew 9:36-10:1

When he looked out over the crowds, his heart broke. So confused and aimless they were, like sheep with no shepherd. "What a huge harvest!" he said to his disciples. "How few workers! On your knees and pray for harvest hands!"

The prayer was no sooner prayed than it was answered. Jesus called twelve of his followers and sent them into the ripe fields. He gave them power to kick out the evil spirits and to tenderly care for the bruised and hurt lives.

Mark 11:25

"And when you assume the posture of prayer, remember that it's not all *asking*. If you have anything against someone, *forgive* — only then will your heavenly Father be inclined to also wipe your slate clean of sins."

1 John 5:15-16

And if we're confident that he's listening, we know that what we've asked for is as good as ours.

For instance, if we see a Christian believer sinning (clearly I'm not talking about those who make a practice of sin in a way that is "fatal," leading to eternal death), we ask for God's help and he gladly gives it, gives life to the sinner whose sin is not fatal.

Mark 7:33-35

He took the man off by himself, put his fingers in the man's ears and some spit on the man's tongue. Then Jesus looked up in prayer, groaned mightily, and commanded, "*Ephphatha!* — Open up!" And it happened. The man's hearing was clear and his speech plain — just like that.

Acts 28:8-9

Publius's father was sick at the time, down with a high fever and dysentery. Paul went to the old man's room, and

when he laid hands on him and prayed, the man was healed.
Word of the healing got around fast, and soon everyone on
the island who was sick came and got healed.

Job 42:9-11

They did it. Eliphaz the Temanite, Bildad the Shuhite, and
Zophar the Naamathite did what GOD commanded. And
GOD accepted Job's prayer.

After Job had interceded for his friends, GOD restored
his fortune — and then doubled it! All his brothers and
sisters and friends came to his house and celebrated. They
told him how sorry they were, and consoled him for all the
trouble GOD had brought him. Each of them brought
generous housewarming gifts.

John 11:41-44

Then, to the others, "Go ahead, take away the stone."
They removed the stone. Jesus raised his eyes to heaven
and prayed, "Father, I'm grateful that you have listened to
me. I know you always do listen, but on account of this
crowd standing here I've spoken so that they might believe
that you sent me."

Then he shouted, "Lazarus, come out!" And he came out, a cadaver, wrapped from head to toe, and with a kerchief over his face.

Jesus told them, "Unwrap him and let him loose."

### Luke 5:12-13

One day in one of the villages there was a man covered with leprosy. When he saw Jesus he fell down before him in prayer and said, "If you want to, you can cleanse me."

Jesus put out his hand, touched him, and said, "I want to. Be clean." Then and there his skin was smooth, the leprosy gone.

### 1 John 1:8-9

If we claim that we're free of sin, we're only fooling ourselves. A claim like that is errant nonsense. On the other hand, if we admit our sins — make a clean breast of them — he won't let us down; he'll be true to himself. He'll forgive our sins and purge us of all wrongdoing.

### James 5:13-19

Are you hurting? Pray. Do you feel great? Sing. Are you sick? Call the church leaders together to pray and anoint you with oil in the name of the Master. Believing-prayer will heal you, and Jesus will put you on your feet. And if you've sinned, you'll be forgiven — healed inside and out.

Make this your common practice: Confess your sins to each other and pray for each other so that you can live together whole and healed. The prayer of a person living right with God is something powerful to be reckoned with. Elijah, for instance, human just like us, prayed hard that it wouldn't rain, and it didn't — not a drop for three and a half years. Then he prayed that it would rain, and it did. The showers came and everything started growing again.

My dear friends, if you know people who have wandered off from God's truth, don't write them off. Go after them. Get them back.

Luke 18:13-14

"Meanwhile the tax man, slumped in the shadows, his face in his hands, not daring to look up, said, 'God, give mercy. Forgive me, a sinner.'"

Jesus commented, "This tax man, not the other, went home made right with God. If you walk around with your nose in the air, you're going to end up flat on your face, but if you're content to be simply yourself, you will become more than yourself."

Job 33:25-27

> "Before you know it, you're healed,
> the very picture of health!"

> "Or, you may fall on your knees and pray — to God's delight!
> You'll see God's smile and celebrate,
> finding yourself set right with God.
> You'll sing God's praises to everyone you meet,
> testifying, 'I messed up my life —
> and let me tell you, it wasn't worth it.'"

Psalm 32:5-6

> Then I let it all out;
> I said, "I'll make a clean breast of my failures to GOD."

> Suddenly the pressure was gone —
> my guilt dissolved,
> my sin disappeared.

These things add up. Every one of us needs to pray;
>   when all hell breaks loose and the dam bursts
>   we'll be on high ground, untouched.

2 Chronicles 6:36-40, *a prayer of Solomon in the Temple*

When they sin against you — and they certainly will; there's
no one without sin! — and in anger you turn them over to
the enemy and they are taken off captive to the enemy's
land, whether far or near, but then repent in the country of
their captivity and pray with changed hearts in their exile,
"We've sinned; we've done wrong; we've been most wicked,"
and they turn back to you heart and soul in the land of the
enemy who conquered them, and pray to you toward their
homeland, the land you gave their ancestors, toward the
city you chose, and this Temple I have built to the honor of
your Name,

Listen from your home in heaven
>   to their prayers desperate and devout;
Do what is best for them.
>   Forgive your people who have sinned against you.

And now, dear God, be alert and attentive to prayer, all prayer, offered in this place.

2 Chronicles 7:14-15, *God's response to Solomon*

"And my people, my God-defined people, respond by humbling themselves, praying, seeking my presence, and turning their backs on their wicked lives, I'll be there ready for you: I'll listen from heaven, forgive their sins, and restore their land to health. From now on I'm alert day and night to the prayers offered at this place."

Psalm 69:29-31

I'm hurt and in pain;
Give me space for healing, and mountain air.

Let me shout God's name with a praising song,
Let me tell his greatness in a prayer of thanks.

For GOD, this is better than oxen on the altar,
Far better than blue-ribbon bulls.

Isaiah 55:6-7

> Seek GOD while he's here to be found,
>     pray to him while he's close at hand.
> Let the wicked abandon their way of life
>     and the evil their way of thinking.
> Let them come back to GOD, who is merciful,
>     come back to our God, who is lavish with forgiveness.

2 Chronicles 20:8-9

> "They have lived here and built a holy house of worship
> to honor you, saying, 'When the worst happens — whether
> war or flood or disease or famine — and we take our place
> before this Temple (we know you are personally present in
> this place!) and pray out our pain and trouble, we know that
> you will listen and give victory.'"

Jonah 2:6-7

> "I was as far down as a body can go,
>     and the gates were slamming shut behind me forever —
> Yet you pulled me up from that grave alive,
>     O GOD, my God!

When my life was slipping away,
    I remembered GOD,
And my prayer got through to you,
      made it all the way to your Holy Temple."

Luke 6:27-29

"To you who are ready for the truth, I say this: Love your
enemies. Let them bring out the best in you, not the worst.
When someone gives you a hard time, respond with the
energies of prayer for that person. If someone slaps you
in the face, stand there and take it. If someone grabs your
shirt, giftwrap your best coat and make a present of it."

Luke 23:34

Jesus prayed, "Father, forgive them; they don't know what
they're doing."

1 Kings 13:6

The king pleaded with the holy man, "Help me! Pray to
your GOD for the healing of my arm." The holy man prayed
for him and the king's arm was healed—as good as new!

*You can be sure that God will take care of everything you need, his generosity exceeding even yours in the glory that pours from Jesus.*

—PHILIPPIANS 4:19

*Then Abraham prayed to God and God healed Abimelech, his wife and his maidservants.*

—GENESIS 20:17

# Prayers *for* the Future

Matthew 21:21-22

> But Jesus was matter-of-fact: "Yes — and if you embrace this kingdom life and don't doubt God, you'll not only do minor feats like I did to the fig tree, but also triumph over huge obstacles. This mountain, for instance, you'll tell, 'Go jump in the lake,' and it will jump. Absolutely everything, ranging from small to large, as you make it a part of your believing prayer, gets included as you lay hold of God."

1 Peter 1:17-22

> You call out to God for help and he helps — he's a good Father that way. But don't forget, he's also a responsible Father, and won't let you get by with sloppy living.
> Your life is a journey you must travel with a deep

consciousness of God. It cost God plenty to get you out of that dead-end, empty-headed life you grew up in. He paid with Christ's sacred blood, you know. He died like an unblemished, sacrificial lamb. And this was no afterthought. Even though it has only lately — at the end of the ages — become public knowledge, God always knew he was going to do this for you. It's because of this sacrificed Messiah, whom God then raised from the dead and glorified, that you trust God, that you know you have a future in God.

Now that you've cleaned up your lives by following the truth, love one another as if your lives depended on it.

## 2 Thessalonians 1:10-12

But on that very same day when he comes, he will be exalted by his followers and celebrated by all who believe — and all because you believed what we told you.

Because we know that this extraordinary day is just ahead, we pray for you all the time — pray that our God will make you fit for what he's called you to be, pray that he'll fill your good ideas and acts of faith with his own energy so that it all amounts to something. If your life honors the name of Jesus, he will honor you. Grace is behind and through all of this, our God giving himself freely, the Master, Jesus Christ, giving himself freely.

Jeremiah 29:11-14

"I know what I'm doing. I have it all planned out — plans to take care of you, not abandon you, plans to give you the future you hope for."

"When you call on me, when you come and pray to me, I'll listen. When you come looking for me, you'll find me."

"Yes, when you get serious about finding me and want it more than anything else, I'll make sure you won't be disappointed."

John 14:13, *the power of praying in Jesus' name*

"From now on, whatever you request along the lines of who I am and what I am doing, I'll do it. That's how the Father will be seen for who he is in the Son. I mean it."

Luke 18:7-8

"What makes you think God won't step in and work justice for his chosen people, who continue to cry out for help?

Won't he stick up for them? I assure you, he will. He will not drag his feet. But how much of that kind of persistent faith will the Son of Man find on the earth when he returns?"

1 John 3:22

We're able to stretch our hands out and receive what we asked for because we're doing what he said, doing what pleases him.

1 Corinthians 11:12-15

The first woman came from man, true — but ever since then, every man comes from a woman! And since virtually everything comes from God anyway, let's quit going through these "who's first" routines.

Don't you agree there is something naturally powerful in the symbolism — a woman, her beautiful hair reminiscent of angels, praying in adoration; a man, his head bared in reverence, praying in submission?

1 Thessalonians 3:9-13

What would be an adequate thanksgiving to offer God for all the joy we experience before him because of you? We do what we can, praying away, night and day, asking for the bonus of seeing your faces again and doing what we can to help when your faith falters.

May God our Father himself and our Master Jesus clear the road to you!

John 17:20-23

"I'm praying not only for them
But also for those who will believe in me
Because of them and their witness about me.
The goal is for all of them to become one heart and mind—
Just as you, Father, are in me and I in you,
So they might be one heart and mind with us.
Then the world might believe that you, in fact, sent me.
The same glory you gave me, I gave them,
So they'll be as unified and together as we are—
I in them and you in me."

Psalm 102:17-20

When he attends to the prayer of the wretched,
    He won't dismiss their prayer.

Write this down for the next generation
　　so people not yet born will praise GOD:
"GOD looked out from his high holy place;
　　from heaven he surveyed the earth.
He listened to the groans of the doomed,
　　he opened the doors of their death cells."

Psalm 145:17-19

Everything GOD does is right —
　　the trademark on all his works is love.

GOD's there, listening for all who pray,
　　for all who pray and mean it.

He does what's best for those who fear him —
　　hears them call out, and saves them.

Mark 13:29-31

"And so it is with you. When you see all these things, you
know he is at the door. Don't take this lightly. I'm not just
saying this for some future generation, but for this one,

too — these things will happen. Sky and earth will wear out; my words won't wear out."

1 Kings 8:58-60, *a blessing from Solomon*

"May he keep us centered and devoted to him, following the life path he has cleared, watching the signposts, walking at the pace and rhythms he laid down for our ancestors."

"And let these words that I've prayed in the presence of GOD be always right there before him, day and night, so that he'll do what is right for me, to guarantee justice for his people Israel day after day after day. Then all the people on earth will know GOD is the true God; there is no other God."

Jude 19–21

These are the ones who split churches, thinking only of themselves. There's nothing to them, no sign of the Spirit!

But you, dear friends, carefully build yourselves up in this most holy faith by praying in the Holy Spirit, staying right at the center of God's love, keeping your arms open and outstretched, ready for the mercy of our Master, Jesus Christ. This is the unending life, the *real* life!

Exodus 33:12-14

> Moses said to GOD, "Look, you tell me, 'Lead this people,' but you don't let me know whom you're going to send with me. You tell me, 'I know you well and you are special to me.' If I am so special to you, let me in on your plans. That way, I will continue being special to you. Don't forget, this is *your* people, your responsibility."
>
> GOD said, "My presence will go with you. I'll see the journey to the end."

*Ask and you'll get;*

*Seek and you'll find;*

*Knock and the door will open.*

*Don't bargain with God. Be direct.*

*Ask for what you need.*

—Luke 11:9-10